The Reaches

poems by

Steve Wilson

Finishing Line Press
Georgetown, Kentucky

The Reaches

Copyright © 2019 by Steve Wilson
ISBN 978-1-64662-096-8 First Edition
All rights reserved under International and Pan-American Copyright Conventions. No part of this book may be reproduced in any manner whatsoever without written permission from the publisher, except in the case of brief quotations embodied in critical articles and reviews.

ACKNOWLEDGMENTS

A number of poems in this collection, some in earlier versions, appeared in the following journals: *Beloit Poetry Journal, Cenizo, Christian Science Monitor,* the "Ekphrastic Poetry" online feature of the Maier Museum of Art at Randolph College, *Ireland of the Welcomes, Louisiana Literature, Midwest Quarterly, New American Writing, Salamander, San Pedro River Review,* and *Texas Observer.*

Publisher: Leah Maines
Editor: Christen Kincaid
Cover Art: George W. Wilson
Author Photo: Connor Wilson
Cover Design: Elizabeth Maines McCleavy

Printed in the USA on acid-free paper.
Order online: www.finishinglinepress.com
also available on amazon.com

Author inquiries and mail orders:
Finishing Line Press
P. O. Box 1626
Georgetown, Kentucky 40324
U. S. A.

Table of Contents

Săracă Inima Mè (My Sorrowing Heart) 1

Throatpoke Triolet 2

The Hunger Bird 3

Light You Eat 4

Zeitgeist Sonnet 5

The gar 6

Galley Head 7

Small Poem for Peter Ramus 8

Turns Toward Spring 9

Tone Study 10

The Basilica at Aquileia 11

Moksha 12

Extravagance 13

Aardwolf 14

Six Versions of the Darkness 15

El Guajiro 16

The Beekeeper 17

The Beauty of the Village 18

Poem for Aretha Franklin 19

Solo Road-Trip West 20

The Supernumeraries 21

Articulated Tram 22

Timoleague Reveries 23

Caoinim 24

Four Winter Haiku 25

À la Tombée de la Nuit 26

On the Alligator 27

Hello 28

Drought 29

Săracă Inima Mè (My Sorrowing Heart)
—outside Biertan, Romania

Hush, my heart. There is still the light

through the windows, fields that remember
you. Past the yellow church beside the forest,
hush. I've had to learn the ease of waiting.
Somewhere, in autumns, the songs grow surer
with waiting. You cannot hurry through
hurt. Quiet. Still. Slow, like those swallows
along the rooftops. Color upon a shawl.

World, loving its long evenings in silence.

Throatpoke Triolet

Bruised but not broken. Lumpished up.
      Someone's sheen, patina
           turned under. Skin was insistent;
bruised, but not. Broken lump. *-ished-up*
        with a slap of syllables—said
          do. Insisted. Throatpoke.
Bruised but not broken. Lumpished up.
Someone's sheen, patina.

The Hunger Bird

At windows, the darker trees, where
the blue-barred wing I understand
sparks and shows against voices,
some cold eye now suddens
within ragged light—lifted, shifting

> on the branches gray, green;
> white shards scattered upon the walk.
> Beneath the slow space of sound imagine
>
> rain—its lulled fall we've wanted long.
> Memory, is that your hand upon the latch?
> Thought, have you taken to hollows?

Here is my need—a crackled call
or syllable that withers the breath: of winter,
blown down pines. She has drifted
toward a certain sleep—deep oak.
Old Soul, for a moment then, know, touch.

Light You Eat

Like winds wound dry. Call it comfort:
      the edge of something sure.
            Watch the waters, sound through squall. Waves
like winds wound dry. Call it comfort
        huddles here. To sit, sing,
        where words have settled—shores,
like winds wound, dry. Call it comfort—
the edge of something sure.

Zeitgeist Sonnet

—I won't dig down—you go dig—you go
ramble—you go do—I won't answer calls
to conscience—missions—transfer—either—
outward—you go dance—you have wish lists—
you make memory—have your heart out—help
with drift—hush and hurry—you go under
all the way through—past—then farther—
I won't steer us—stall us—strangle chance
because of history—I won't speak it—you say
tremble—you say *buck up*—you say follow—
you feel—you fail—you drop leaflets over
jungles burned by hungry—trees of passion—
   vines of treaties—you tongue roots—where roots
   tap trouble you confuse—construe—you try true—

The gar

Fronts that whip-
saw of teeth—

Drifts beneath the green
cabomba, a skeleton—

Looms near the shallows—

Undulates
like a snake, reverberates
against ripples—

Grays, as if an abandoned shadow—

Offers its silvery skin to the sunlight—

Lazes beside
currents, deeper waters—

Endures even beyond the chill
nothingnesses of winter—

Asks nothing, gives
nothing, settles
and quiets—

Brushes against the submerged cypress trunks—

Coaxes its fellows from the darks within
the reed banks—

Stills, then
stills again—

Reminds silt
of its sifting—

Galley Head

I know myself. I know my mind—
    the riffling tidal lights
        that, settled by the evening, slow.
I know. Myself I know. My mind
        a cove—shore by shadow undone:
        it darks, and dies, and dies.
I know myself. I know my mind—
    the riffling tidal lights.

Small Poem for Peter Ramus

　　　　　　　　　　　　　　I. Yes, I. I'd break

　　　　　　　　　　against dark for the hope
　　　　　　　　　　it shapes—a window's warp,

　　　　　　　　　as if wave shuddered toward
　　　　　　　　　　　water. I'd slash and turn.

　　　　　　　　Swim jungle floods, then down.
　　　　　　　　Augur toward some thin-rilled

　　　　　　　space—this world—where skin is
　　　　　　　ache, where else we'd wish for
　　　　　　　　words that perfect hold us.

Turns Toward Spring

—a long walk
through this gray morning. Sounds
take shape—

      ***

White clouds cradle
in the bowl of the valley.

      ***

Clear days
upon clear. Spring thoughts rattle
the salvia stalks.

Tone Study

Within the weary beauty of Chopin—
nonpareils, Champagne—we sit and sit,
confused accoutrements. Monet, who dreamed
of water: how unbodied do his lights
descend. And small Gauguin consumed like sweets
his nudes, his mangoes, greens, the girls unsure
he'd keep his word. To wander slow, dead slow,
along ennui. Ah, the luxuriousness of boredom.
Sea breeze. A certain way of shaping sound
and color. And music. Long, retiring chords—say
the way is clearer now, my friends, friends for
the polonaise. Insistent, nonchalant,
we're languorous in time. I'd turn. I would,
but for the weakened battlements outside.

The Basilica at Aquileia

From blue confusions—of current,
        whirl, fishheart, old dread sea—
from blue confusions of current
            he swims himself sure. Air
            a landscape. Stone, his mind,
from blue. Confusions of current
whirl: fishheart, old dread, sea.

Moksha
    —for Geetanjali

          gray light
      through the garden window, late

afternoon—

          storms blossom
      over the ridge, within darkening

            clouds—I watch
   myself watching

Extravagance
   —*for Robert Creeley*

like a numbing thumb,
the moment dulls until it tastes
complicity. Of worry

then the crawing gnaw—to eat and eat is all,
is all. I've stored long
loss upon some kitchen shelf.

A jar that rounds along
the night. Worry words: that works
us sure, the way

a nightbird sures—through shadow sures
its call. At least
this once. This one, at last.

Aardwolf

—hurry slinkskunk, earthdog—down
to dirt—and dig—you now cowered within

brown grasses—underground and sured—

from your hollows wait for day—its wander
over the plains—how to sense some shift

inside—how to claw this open and how to find

—to eat and eat and eat—listen—your dark
call—your turn away so clever sidestep—

shadows—heat alive to light—the hard sun—

Six Versions of the Darkness

All night, rains flood the draws
near Purgatory Creek, surge
through our dreams.

                ***

My questions for the gods
tonight (moon mirrored in river):
What is? Whose?

                ***

A lover of shadows, I
patrol these sleepless nights.

                ***

Tonight's unease tunneled out,
not down—
the olive trees' shallowing roots.

                ***

The night cracks open,
—lightning and wild winds—
spring resisting summer.

                ***

we lose count,
our place—the dark
night thrums

El Guajiro
—after Guillermo Portabales

Like a breeze from the plains, deliciously weary,
the *tres* coaxes him down slow roads. He remembers:
trees, the ocean as it lows—they are lovers always
departing. Yes, always asking. How far to Mayari?
Even so? With his mother's evening voice, this night—
how it speaks sure the words he'd forgotten long—
some boy unschooled, new to the world and secrets.

The Beekeeper
    —*Adlesic, Slovenia*

Summer comes luscious as amber and honey.

It flows up from willow roots, the rushes' dead stalks—
a hum soft under sound—to whisper the fields awake.
It floats within wind-rivers shaped from prairie grasses.

Borne upon bees' wings, the days are sweetened to fullness.
Suddenly, in the orchard the greenest suggestions—new
leaves—try the light, urging the trees' black branches.

No surprise, then, to see bees leave their hives. They'll linger
and linger along the white of pear blossoms: a white, perfumed,
that through the village goes, quick with warmth,

even down to the stilled, chill shadows of the forest.

The Beauty of the Village
   —after a painting by Theodore Clement Steele

—along the hills,
the broadening crowns
of maples. Autumn,

and a few leaves
early gone.
Even to the edge of sight,

the sky worries its moments
of blue and white,
bluewhite, green.

The valley, barns
and their dark houses—
therein happens some old concern:

thought now, it settles,
a shadow,
in some farther room—

Poem for Aretha Franklin

                      Perhaps, as a consolation, beauty is
        distance, opening—
as it wanders, sometimes

it traces the dunes
                    of a white shore bordered by shadow.
            Others, like a dark road

it coaxes us
beyond ourselves and out
                        into the fields

now fallow
below those first greening
hills.

Solo Road-Trip West

An hour outside Ozona,
only the marbled

stanzas of scrubland
below the mesas.

The interminable, perfect
sky—its confidences.

What's always been,
and nothing more.

The Supernumeraries

Offstage, they've seen it all before, the final scene
that calls them from their friendly game of cards.

Someone will be murdered tonight. The count,
foreign-born, sings of a dream: a woman,

alluring behind her green mask, offers wine
to her secret lover. It is a persuasive shade of red.

When he drinks, nightjars scatter for the forest.
It is an omen the count cannot ignore. Who will believe?

Who will take from his hand jewels bound in a kerchief
that would save the beautiful soprano? He thinks

the watery curve of her whispers is a revelation.
Curious, how his life is mirrored in music. A light

from somewhere in the wings, upon the swells
of violins. The morning he feared would arrive.

That growing tide of chord upon chord. . . . Yes,
someone will be murdered—there's a dagger

in the folds of the diplomat's cloak. Done
since Act Two, while voices swirl like leaves

the courier clowns in his Stetson stage left, signaling
beers all round. The coachman places his bet.

Articulated Tram

By basement filigrees, the intricate particulars of passageways.
By looklongs in bank lobbies that lead to suspicions unresolved.
By alleys, lumbered with their Chinese restaurants, hung ducks,
    trouble-me packets—instant noodles.
By the dressmaker who sells stolen watches from her balcony because.
By the gypsy family who work the sidewalk where scents last,
    linger—ginger, Turkish coffee—just past opera crowds.
By a roman face surprised in the wall of a house. The butcher
    used the stall downstairs until police last summer
    roughed him up. His hands knew. His hands revealed
    sinews sublime with design.
By cocktail seminars—down-shops, really—where argument
    keeps seeping along the hallway.
By apartment blocs, whose weariness charms—think of such
    intrigues of the window-frame as it crumbles, its little
    cracks the cracks tracing through an old woman's
    memory.
By accidents, held to one's self, the suggestions.
By the equestrian statue luring, revolutions that finally won't
    matter.
By bookstores whose shelves display confused appliances.
    Toasters from Singapore. One curling iron. Leon Uris'
    monolithic *Trinity*.
By yellowgreen or purple houses—the elaborate wooden gates—
    still sobering under the sun.
By a briefcase and Italian suit.
By the ruins, remade. That stone, is it a widow's shawl? Her
    shadow looms still like the breath of a gesture.

With your permission, I will rise and note her going.

Timoleague Reveries

Timoleague's red houses, green, yellow,
along the strand—a testament of gray
boulders—huddled
against the sea's incessant swells.

***

Low tide near noon. The mud flats,
astir with birds (oystercatchers,
avocets, a few bumbling gulls),
steam and sheen beneath
the brilliant summer sun.

***

Psalm for our silences:
the ragged calls of crows echo
down the quay, the ruined friary walls.

***

Arpeggiated lanes, a cacophony
of church bells—shadows
(lengthening, angular) amble
toward the sea.

Caoinim

                From within
old darknesses,

              wind—bone-
                     raw with winter—
soughs through shadow,

the bare trees.

Four Winter Haiku

What is this other
        that whispers us
toward night, its falling?

    *

Sometimes the gray of trees.
        Sometimes only water,
because it moves.

    *

Would have found you
        if I'd looked
—there are always more poems.

    *

Imagine a winterway, distance—
        slow roads that end,
undone, in shadow.

    *

À la Tombée de la Nuit

To breathe—a heaviness.
The body settling into a chair

before the TV, watching
as one by one they fall:
in their offices, at schools,

on their way home from the shops.
Like some shifting of shadows

in a park, or the way winter languishes
above the frozen pond, it wearies,
this gray futility, as the evening

along the somber boulevards
ever deepens and expands.

On the Alligator

—days is teeth—teeth
and stone that's skin—

and an eye looking through

to the cash in the purse—
days is a black confession

gone buried for months

out back by the shed—where
the grass browns—already down

from this winter—or birds

hunker hard in bare trees
above the banks of the bayou—

days is days is what—

Hello

and flower stalls and the city park
the market near the taxi stand
tomatoes melons bluesky ice cream

and toward the trains the round white clock
and the stadium three boys testing kicks
children climbing stairs to schoolrooms

the swirl of squares of people going
sitting at cafes buying magazines
stopping to read catch the tram

gestures across the lanes the sudden
bridge and the rise toward the church
and all at once and everything yes everything

Drought

Bone-dry,
dead ocotillos
rasp and rattle

in the desert winds, brittle
down to the roots.

Recent poems by **Steve Wilson** are out or forthcoming in such journals as *Beloit Poetry Journal, Borderlands, Bluestem, Rio Grande Review, Cimarron Review, Commonweal, Poem, Georgetown Review, North American Review, America, The Christian Science Monitor, Blue Unicorn, New Orleans Review, San Pedro River Review, The Christian Century, New American Writing, Isotope: A Journal of Literary Nature and Science Writing, Midwest Quarterly, The Rio Grande Review,* and *New Letters;* as well as in a number of anthologies, including *O Taste and See: Food Poems* (Bottom Dog Press), *Visiting Frost: Poems Inspired by Robert Frost* (University of Iowa), *Stories from Where We Live: The Gulf Coast* (Milkweed Editions), *Like Thunder: Poets Respond to Violence in America* (University of Iowa), *What Have You Lost?* (Greenwillow), *American Diaspora: Poetry of Displacement* (University of Iowa), *An Introduction to the Prose Poem* (Firewheel Editions), *Beloved on the Earth: 150 Poems of Grief and Gratitude* (Holy Cow! Press), *Classifieds: An Anthology of Prose Poems* (Equinox), *Improbable Worlds: An Anthology of Texas and Louisiana Poets* (Mutabilis) and *Going Down Grand: Poetry of the Grand Canyon* (Lithic). His books include *Allegory Dance,* **The Singapore Express,** *The Lost Seventh,* and *Lose to Find.*

www.ingramcontent.com/pod-product-compliance
Lightning Source LLC
LaVergne TN
LVHW041514070426
835507LV00012B/1555